AROUND
BATH
IN OLD PHOTOGRAPHS

NOAD'S BAKERY, Frome Road, around 1935. Henry James Noad and Dorothy (known as Darby) Noad are shown standing out side. The Noad family have been baking at Odd Down for over 140 years. The Frome Road shop was pulled down and replaced by Gateway supermarket in 1965 and Noad's new bakers shop was built around the corner.

Front Cover Illustration:

THE TURNPIKE, NEWTON ST LOE, at the fork between Upper and Lower Bristol Roads. This cottage stood there for 150 years before being demolished around 1969.

AROUND
BATH
IN OLD PHOTOGRAPHS

COLLECTED BY
PETER JONES

ALAN SUTTON

Alan Sutton Publishing Limited
Phoenix Mill · Far Thrupp · Stroud · Gloucestershire

First Published 1991

British Library Cataloguing in Publication Data

Around Bath in old photographs.
I. Jones, Peter, *1940*
942.398

ISBN 0-86299-906-5

Typeset in 9/10 Korinna.
Typesetting and origination by
Alan Sutton Publishing Limited.
Printed in Great Britain by
The Bath Press, Avon.

CONTENTS

DEDICATION: to my wife Joan for her help and patience.

MOUNT ROAD, SOUTHDOWN around 1910. The Sladebrook Gospel Hall on the left was built in 1904. The shops have now been converted to dwelling houses.

INTRODUCTION AND ACKNOWLEDGEMENTS

The compilation of this book has satisfied a yearning to share some of my collection of photographs with other interested people. Many of the photographs are unique and may only be seen within these pages.

My interest in the history of Bath started around 1970 when I was awakened to the sack of the city and realized that some areas had changed forever; I wanted to find out what these areas were like before the changes began. The Georgian buildings, Bath Abbey, Milsom Street, High Street and the Roman Baths were not a problem as the bookshops and libraries contain much on them. When I looked for information about the lesser known streets of Bath and the areas skirting the city I found a different story. Books written by local historians did not have many photographs, other than those of churches or the manor houses of surrounding villages, so I searched local antique shops for old photographs and discovered that picture postcards were the best way to find out about local history.

Most postcards tell a story. Not many photograhic cards date from before 1902, which was the great Edwardian collecting era, so there are limitations on how far back we can go with the postcard, and from 1850 to 1900 photographs are difficult to identify as they are rarely captioned. Sometimes the name of the photographer printed on the back or front of the photograph is the only clue as to its whereabouts. But virtually every road, street, avenue or event was photographed for posterity and we have a good record of our area in the last ninety years. These were usually published and sold at local stores. Will collectors be able to find such interesting photographs or postcards of our present day in ninety years time? I fear not, except perhaps for the usual views of the glorious Georgian buildings of Bath, pictures of which are still sent all over the world.

The changes we can see in areas where housing estates have been built or buildings have been demolished makes some pictures worth a closer look. Other scenes, like those taken of Oldfield Park, have changed very little. Many of the buildings were quite new at the time the photographs were taken. The blitz of the Second World War took its toll on the areas around Bath as well as the city itself. Many of the buildings which were bombed were rebuilt to a more modern design, others were constructed as close to the original as possible.

Not all the areas around Bath have been covered in this book, but I hope the ones which have been included will provide the reader with as much enjoyment as I have had in compiling the book.

I would like to acknowledge help I have received from Colin Maggs, Duncan Harper, the *Bath Evening Chronicle*, Bath Reference Library, Kelly's Directories and Frith's. My thanks to Mike Tozer and Mike Burns for the use of their photographs.

Peter Jones

SECTION ONE

Weston

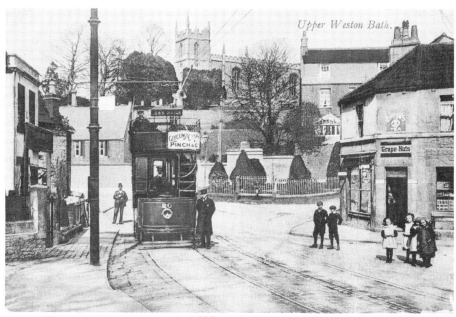

THE NO. 20 TRAM IN WESTON VILLAGE in 1903, ready to go to its destination, the GWR station. Early guide books described Weston as a village of washerwomen. In 1865 there were sixty-five laundresses listed in the village. Weston was divided into 'Upper' and 'Lower' in 1879, and was completely taken into the city boundary after the Second World War.

WESTON VILLAGE, seen from the opposite direction before the village by-pass was built. P.H. Day's dairy is in the centre.

WESTON HIGH STREET around 1912.

WESTON WAR MEMORIAL in the 1920s, with Crown Hill on the left and a sweet shop on the corner, now replaced by a new block of houses.

WESTON HIGH STREET, from the opposite end to the above photo, in 1911. The Queen's Head, now closed, is on the left.

THE CROWN AND ANCHOR, Weston in 1902. Proprietor J. Adams.

THE WESTON TRAM leaving the village for the GWR station in 1904.

NEWBRIDGE ROAD around 1905. Pictured above is the junction with Station Road by the florists shop pictured below. This was run by H. Parfitt from 1920 to 1928.

CORK PLACE, Weston in 1904

F. MARSH, NEWSAGENT AND TOBACCONIST, No. 3 Cork Place, shown with a large array of advertising in around 1908.

SHAFTESBURY AVENUE, Weston in 1905. Locksbrook Cemetery is at the top.

OSBORNE ROAD, Weston in 1906.

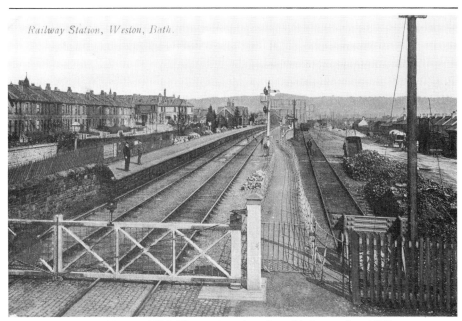

Railway Station, Weston, Bath.

WESTON RAILWAY STATION in 1906. The station closed on 21 September 1953.

Station Rd., Weston, Bath. 921.

STATION ROAD, Weston in around 1912. Note the level crossing gates behind the group of children.

ASHLEY AVENUE, Weston in around 1912. The postcard is captioned 'Aubrey Avenue, Weston'.

A TREE-LINED KENNINGTON ROAD, Weston in 1906.

NEWBRIDGE ROAD, Weston in 1906. The Weston Hotel is on the left. Children are taking a rest from playing with their hoops. The tram is on its way to Weston.

PARK ROAD, Weston around 1905. Hooper's newsagents advertises *Tit-Bits* magazine and a £500 prize which was a fortune at this time.

WESTON ALL SAINTS' FOOTBALL TEAM, winners of the Bath City Junior Knock-Out Cup, 1908/09. Back row, left to right: ? Burford, F. Helps, H. Podger, H. Cross, G. Smith, T. Topping, J. Ball, W. Lovell, E. Mortimer. Second row: J. Humphries, R. Barnes, F. Wadsworth, W. Anstey, W. Smith, W. Morley. Front row: H. Wilkins, E. Cross.

WESTON DAIRY around 1908. Smartly dressed dairymen and well polished milk churns.

CHELSEA ROAD, Weston around 1904. The delivery boys are having a rest and a telegraph boy poses in the centre.

TRAFALGAR ROAD, Weston in 1904. Pointings Brewery is on the left.

HUNGERFORD ROAD, Weston around 1904.

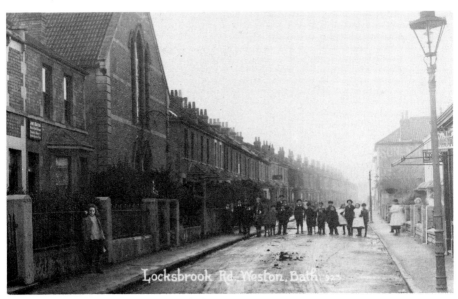

LOCKSBROOK ROAD, Weston around 1912.

Foxcombe Road, Weston, Bath.

FOXCOMBE ROAD, Weston around 1906.

WESTON in around 1904. There is no shortage of children for the camera.

COMBE PARK, Weston around 1912.

PENN LEA ROAD, Weston around 1914.

BATH WAR HOSPITAL FOOTBALL TEAM at Combe Park, 1918/19. Bill Jones, my father, is standing third from left.

Bath War Hospital. 1915.
Ward No 8.

ONE OF THE MANY WARDS AT THE BATH WAR HOSPITAL, c. 1915. The hospital was erected by the War Office in 1915 after it had chosen Bath as the site for an additional hospital for wounded soldiers. Originally designed for 505 patients, the War Hospital was so successful that, at the request of the authorities, it was increased to 1,250 beds, bringing the accommodation, with auxiliaries, to about 1,500 beds.

Twerton

SOUTH VIEW ROAD, TWERTON decorated for the coronation of George V, 22 June 1911.

VERNON PARK, Twerton around 1905.

W. AND R. COOK, WHOLESALE CLOTHIER, started in Twerton in 1891 and traded until around 1960.

TWERTON FERRY, which closed on 7 April 1906. It was officially called the Royal Old Ferry.

TWERTON STATION around 1905, with a view up the High Street. The station closed in 1917. The name Twerton was interpreted by Professor Earle as meaning the town at the Weir or possibly the Weaver's town. In 1790 it consisted of one street about half a mile in length, and the house known as Fielding Lodge was the first on the right from Bath. Henry Fielding, the author of *Tom Jones*, lived there for some time. The house has now been demolished for road improvements.

TWERTON HIGH STREET around 1905, looking towards the station with a footbridge over the railway.

TWERTON HIGH STREET around 1905, looking in the opposite direction. The post office is on the corner of Mill Lane.

RAILWAY BUILDINGS in 1912. The Railway Hotel is on the left and Batten's grocery store on the corner.

CHARABANC OUTING from the Seven Stars, Twerton in the 1920s.

TWERTON PAROCHIAL SCHOOL, 1907.

A LARGE CLASSROOM AT TWERTON PAROCHIAL SCHOOL photographed a few years earlier.

THE OFFICIAL OPENING OF INNOX PARK, Twerton by Thomas Carr, the mill owner, in 1909.

TWERTON DRUG STORES at No. 10, Charlton Buildings. C.H. Davies was proprietor from 1924 to 1931.

A VERY NARROW SHOPHOUSE LANE, Twerton around 1910.

A DELIVERY OF BEER BARRELS at the Old Crown Hotel, Twerton around 1908.

LANSDOWN VIEW, TWERTON around 1912. This terrace was built in the late Victorian era.

TWERTON BOAT HOUSE around 1910. Until recently it was used as a scrap yard.

SOUTH TWERTON SCHOOLS, situated at the bottom of Coronation Avenue, in around 1912. Ascension church is next to the schools.

THE ELEMENTARY SCHOOLS, Twerton around 1912. The foundation stone was laid by Jonathan Carr, the mill owner and brother of Thomas Carr (p. 34), on 19 December 1910.

ST BARNABAS' CHURCH, Twerton Hill around 1907. A temporary mission hall stood on this site at the bottom of Rush Hill until the church was built in 1903. A much larger church was built in 1958 next to the Church Hall in Southdown, and the Rush Hill one was demolished.

EAST TWERTON COUNCIL SCHOOL around 1905. The waste ground is now part of the Bath Press.

TWERTON in around 1900. Has the fire brigade been called out to support the falling trees?

EAST TWERTON in around 1905. The Newbridge Inn on the corner has now been demolished.

TWERTON UNION CLUB, situated at No. 15 St Peters Terrace, in around 1906.

THE SCHOOLS Twerton, around 1912, with the railway station entrance on the right.

ST PETER'S TERRACE, Twerton around 1910. The Twerton Co-operative Society shops dominate the scene. They were amalgamated with the Bath society in 1922.

Oldfield Park and Wellsway

C. E. VINER, BAKERS IN OLDFIELD PARK. They were here from 1916 to 1955. The van is decorated for a carnival procession.

MAYFIELD ROAD, Oldfield Park around 1909.

ST KILDAS ROAD, Oldfield Park around 1912.

CYNTHIA ROAD, Oldfield Park, served by single-decker trams from August 1905.

HERBERT ROAD, Oldfield Park around 1912.

RINGWOOD ROAD, Oldfield Park around 1909.

WEST AVENUE, Oldfield Park around 1904.

MILLMEAD ROAD, Oldfield Park around 1909, with the brickyard chimneys in the background. Note the stationers shop and Victoria Hotel on the left of the picture.

STANLEY ROAD, Oldfield Park around 1910. A coal delivery cart is shown on the left.

MAYBRICK ROAD, Oldfield Park around 1912.

BECKHAMPTON ROAD, Oldfield Park around 1905. Durley Park dairy is on the corner. It is used as a sports equipment shop today.

SOUTH AVENUE, Oldfield Park around 1910.

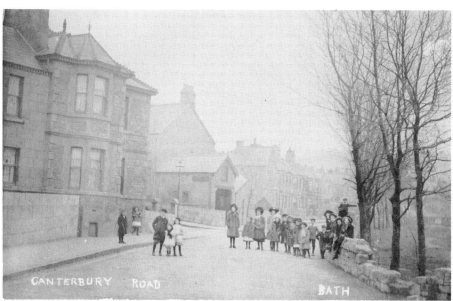

CANTERBURY ROAD, Oldfield Park around 1905. The group of children are well wrapped up in their winter coats.

THE GREAT WESTERN RAILWAY at Oldfield Park. The last steam locomotives to run through Bath on the GWR were in 1965.

A LADY WITH A BASKET selling her wares in Winchester Road, Oldfield Park around 1905.

Triangle & Stanley Rd, Oldfield Park, Bath.

TRIANGLE AND STANLEY ROAD. Oldfield Park around 1907. Note the milk delivery cart on the left of the picture.

OLDFIELD PARK BAPTIST CHAPEL around 1905.

Moorland Rd., Oldfield Park, Bath.

MOORLAND ROAD, Oldfield Park around 1906. The single-decker tram passes the end of the road where some new buildings are being erected.

PICKEN'S BAZAAR AND STORES traded at 49–50 Moorland Road from 1907 to 1909.

THIRD AVENUE, Oldfield Park around 1906. The corner shop belonged to A.S. Boswell. A gas and oil engineers workshop is seen at the end of the avenue.

CHAUCER ROAD around 1915.

MOORLAND ROAD around 1906. The Livingstone Hotel on the right was bombed in the Second World War and rebuilt in a different position in Moorland Road.

WELLS ROAD around 1905, with the tram on its way right through to Bathford, via the city centre.

TWO VIEWS OF WELLSWAY in around 1914, looking both ways.

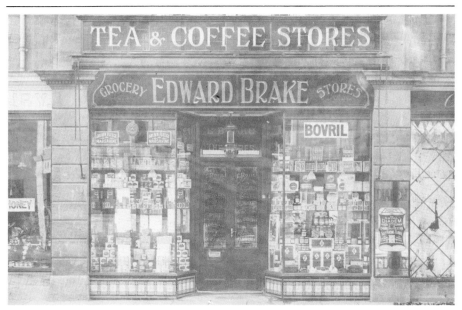

EDWARD BRAKE'S SHOP at No. 4 Wellsway around 1930. It was bombed during the Second World War when F.J. Temlett was the proprietor.

THE BEAR INN, with its horse trough in front, in around 1910. The sign was painted by a Mr Cross who was reputed to paint better when he had had a few drinks.

A HORSE TROUGH BEING ERECTED in Wellsway in 1906. It was donated by Major Brickman.

KIPLING AVENUE around 1906.

SECTION FOUR

Widcombe and Lyncombe

WIDCOMBE around 1908.

Widcombe, Bath, from Beechen Cliff.

WIDCOMBE photographed from Beechen Cliff around 1920. The Dolemeads are shown on the left. Note the gasometer in the centre of the picture.

FOUNDRY PLACE, which was in the slum area of the Dolemeads. The Dolemeads was extensively damaged during the blitz of April 1942 and what remained of some of the old terraced houses was eventually demolished after the war. Situated near the river, this area was continually being flooded before the Avon flood scheme was implemented in the 1970s.

HOLLOWAY around 1902. A busy area down the hill leading to the city.

A VIEW OVER THE DOLEMEADS AND CRICKET GROUND, Widcombe, around 1908.

THE RING OF BELLS BREWERY, Widcombe Parade around 1902. This was run by James Dury from 1894 until 1914.

THE LOCKS AT WIDCOMBE around 1908. Waterloo Buildings on the right was demolished for a road scheme in 1969 and the restoration of the locks was completed in 1976.

FURTHER UP THE CANAL FROM WIDCOMBE around 1912, with the chimney of the upper pumping station on the left.

AN EARLY PHOTOGRAPH OF WIDCOMBE HILL in around 1900. Stockden and Morgan, Coal Merchants and Fly Proprietors, are trading from Widcombe Wharf on the left.

LYNCOMBE VALE, hidden behind Widcombe. This beautiful area is often overlooked by visitors and by local Bath residents as well.

Walcot

LONDON STREET, WALCOT in around 1904. The row of shops was rebuilt in 1900. In the early nineteenth century Walcot was the largest parish in England outside London. It was absorbed into Bath under new local government acts of the mid-nineteenth century.

CLEVELAND BRIDGE in around 1912. All of the buildings on the left, colleges, pharmacies, etc, were connected with the medical profession.

FREEING OF THE CLEVELAND BRIDGE TOLL, 20 July 1929. The single-span cast iron bridge was first opened in September 1827. Ministry of Transport regulations required the bridge to be strengthened, and in 1929 the toll was lifted and the bridge reopened by Lord Bath.

WALCOT PARADE, built in the late eighteenth century, was first known as St Swithun's Terrace and Butler's Buildings.

A GROUP OF CHILDREN at the bottom of Clarence Street around 1905. The banner says 'The Walcot Children's –?– Mission', which was probably run from the church in Thomas Street. The area where the children are standing has since been developed.

A. Glisson, Commission Agent, 11 London Street, Bath.
Telephone 475.   F. G. Goodall, Bath.

A. GLISSON'S VEGETABLE SHOP at 11 London Street, Walcot in 1904.

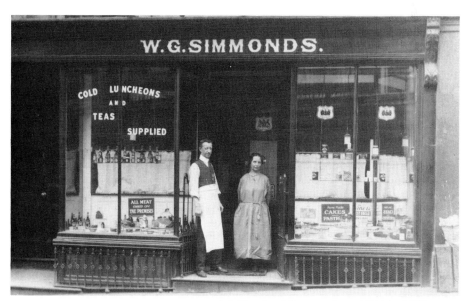

W. G. SIMMONDS' REFRESHMENT ROOMS was at 5 Cleveland Terrace from 1924 to 1953.

A TRAM AT HEDGEMEAD PARK around 1906. The park opened in July 1889 after the landslide of 1875 at Somerset Buildings.

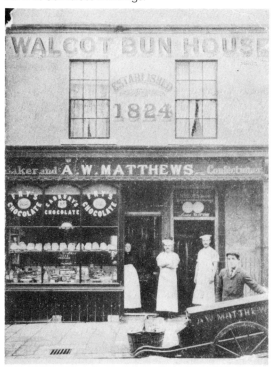

THE WALCOT BUN HOUSE at Walcot Buildings around 1904.

SECTION SIX

Bathwick

BATHWICK STREET from the end of Cleveland Bridge around 1907. Bathwick was a 'wick', or village near Bath, until around 1810. In 1765 the area was inherited by the wife of Sir William Johnstone and assumed the name of Pulteney. Their only child, Henrietta Laura, died in 1808 and it passed to the first Duke of Cleveland. It was bequeathed by the fourth Duke to Captain Forester. This accounts for many of the street names in the parish.

BATHWICK STREET around 1904. The Crown Inn has very little growth over it.

THIS PICTURE shows the Crown Inn a few years later, almost covered by growth.

A BARGE MOVING UP THE CANAL at Sydney Buildings in around 1921.

BATHWICK HILL around 1904.

CLEVELAND BATHS, built in 1815. The baths were filled by spring water from Bathampton Downs and the water was always very cold. It is currently used as a trout farm.

THE BOATING STATION, known locally as Maynards, around 1904. Rowing boats, punts and canoes could be hired to go up to Bathampton Weir. The boating station is still open today.

Larkhall and Grosvenor

LARKHALL in around 1885. Young's butchers shop was situated here until 1889. The right-hand corner shop had not been built at this time. The Larkhall Inn was originally a manor house and was officially declared an inn, where there was stabling for horses and coaches and rest for travellers, in 1784.

THE VIEW OVER LARKHALL around 1912. The changes that have taken place are worth a close look. The brick building in the left foreground has gone and the infants' school is now situated there. More houses have been built on the larges spaces in Larkhall Place, the second row of houses in the centre of the photograph, and the St Saviour's school extensions now stand to the left of these.

LARKHALL SCOUT GROUP MARCHING BAND, pictured in Beaufort Mews in 1911.

LARKHALL in around 1910. The present day Co-op, on the left of the picture, was a drapers and stationers shop run by J. Barter and Company.

LARKHALL in around 1912. Lannings' shoe repair shop on the left was built around 1890. The White Lion Inn is on the right.

ST SAVIOUR'S ROAD around 1912. Note the road surfacing taking place and the steam-roller in the background. On the right is St Saviour's church, which was completed in 1832. St Saviour's became an independent parish in 1840, and with more and more activities, such as weddings and christenings, centred around the church the village of Larkhall started to expand.

CLAREMONT ROAD around 1906. The pillar on the corner is one of many in the area marking the proposed boundary of Worcester Square in the early nineteenth century. Another square, to be called Hanover Square, was also planned but neither were ever built.

DAFFORDS STREET on VE Day. Left to right: S. Hook, B. Nicholls, P. Smith, Joe Jennings, M. Jennings, M. Coombes (hidden), -?-, Curly Cooper, P. Jennings, J. Davis, G. Hook, D. Osborne, P. Davis.

BROOKLYN ROAD, 1945. Mrs Cooper and Mrs Davis stand in the garden. At the bottom of the hill can be seen the Spa Mission Hall built in 1834. The hall was demolished around 1972.

GROSVENOR SUSPENSION BRIDGE around 1905. The houses were demolished and replaced with a block of flats which is called Hampton House.

GROSVENOR SUSPENSION BRIDGE, erected in 1830, was replaced by the present stone bridge in 1929.

GROSVENOR, viewed from Warminster Road around 1905. The steam train is heading out of Bath. St Saviour's church can be seen towering above Grosvenor Place in the centre.

GROSVENOR PLACE around 1912, thickly populated with trees. It was built in 1790 by John Eveleigh.

A HORSE-DRAWN TRAM AT GROSVENOR in 1885. This service started in 1880 and could carry eighteen passengers as far as Southgate Street until replaced by the electric trams in 1904.

LONDON ROAD around 1915, showing a No. 30 tram heading for Bath.

LONDON ROAD, Kensington around 1906.

WILLIAM PRICE'S GREENGROCERY AND POULTRY SHOP at No. 6 Balustrade. He also ran a fishmongers shop at Nos 3 and 4 Balustrade.

ICE SKATING ON KENSINGTON MEADOWS in 1914.

Fairfield, Lansdown and Charlcombe

CAMDEN ROAD in around 1915.

BELGRAVE CRESCENT, off Camden around 1906.

CAMDEN ROAD around 1906.

VIEW FROM CAMDEN OVER GROSVENOR AND LARKHALL around 1912.

MALVERN BUILDINGS, Fairfield around 1908.

RICHMOND PLACE around 1930. The towers of the Royal School appear in the background.

SPRINGFIELD PLACE, LANSDOWN ROAD around 1930. These buildings stood opposite St Stephen's church.

A GATHERING OF CHILDREN AT BEACON HILL around 1905.

ST STEPHEN'S CHURCH in around 1912. A Bath bus, registration number FB 05, is heading for the city centre.

LOOKING OVER CHARLCOMBE in around 1906.

CHARLCOMBE CHURCH around 1906. The writer, Henry Fielding, married his first wife, Sarah, in this church in 1734.

SECTION NINE

Swainswick

LOWER SWAINSWICK around 1950. The post office, which now stands on its own, was part of Gloucester Buildings, of which nineteen houses were demolished for council house development.

SPA GARDENS around 1938. The Bladud's Head is on the right.

FERNDALE ROAD, Swainswick around 1950. A council house estate now stands on the right.

A VIEW OF BAILBROOK around 1920, with Bailbrook House standing out on the right.

EDMONDS' DELIVERY CART around 1909, at their market gardens in Rose Hill, Lower Swainswick. Mr Edmonds is in the driving seat and his young son standing by.

LOOKING OVER BAILBROOK FROM WOOLLEY LANE in 1937. Many new houses, standing out white and clean, were built at Lower Swainswick around this time.

A VIEW OF WOOLLEY VILLAGE from the Gloucester Road around 1936.

Batheaston

BATHEASTON in around 1905. The shops on the left are no longer there, having been replaced by a petrol station.

Bathampton Weirs,
Bath. 1199

BATHEASTON MILL around 1908 before the fire of 1909 which completely destroyed it.

THE OLD FLOUR MILL was reduced to a burnt out shell. The miller at the time was Mr John Elston. The fire was discovered at 2.45 a.m. on 14 November 1909 but, to judge from its intensity, must have been burning for some time, and very high winds carried the smoke over the city. The horse-drawn fire engine arrived at 3.20 a.m. and firemen fought the blaze until after midday. The eight horses stabled at the mill were all led to safety. Mill fires were a common occurrence, Bathampton Mill having been burnt down fourteen years before.

THE OLD MILL was rebuilt as a hotel and restaurant, with a function room at the side. The toll-house and bridge on the left were built in 1872. Before this the only way across was by ferry.

BATHEASTON in around 1908. The White Lion Inn is entirely covered by creeper.

BATHEASTON around 1912, looking towards Bath.

A WIDER VIEW OF THE SAME AREA, with the baker's delivery cart outside the bakers shop.

THE LAMB BREWERY, known as the Lamb and Flag, around 1908. It was closed in 1962 and demolished in 1968.

THE DEDICATION OF THE WAR MEMORIAL at Batheaston church in 1920.

Batheaston.

BATHEASTON VILLAGE in around 1912.

SECTION ELEVEN

Bathampton

BATHAMPTON WEIR AND OLD FLOUR MILL. For many years this century it was a tea garden, with changing rooms and diving boards provided by the tea gardens for swimming in the river. In the 1960s the Keel Club was opened by Keith Johnson. It is now the Beefeater Restaurant.

BATHAMPTON VILLAGE in around 1915.

BATHAMPTON POST OFFICE which was at Court Leet, in around 1902.

THE CANAL AND GEORGE INN, Bathampton around 1915. In the background Harbutt's Plasticine Factory can be seen on the canal bank. It was in production from 1900 to 1983.

THE SWING BRIDGE ON THE CANAL around 1912. It has now been replaced by a footbridge high enough for boats to pass under. The advertising boards on the left are for the Grosvenor Brewery, known as the Folly, situated below the bank. The Folly was burnt down in the Second World War.

MEN FROM THE BATH WAR HOSPITAL AT COMBE PARK were pictured at Harbutt's on Armistice Day 1918 while convalescing at Bathampton House. (See p. 26.)

THE DRY ARCH on The Warminster Road around 1910. It was built to carry Ralph Allen's railway down to the canal for transporting stone into Bath from his quarries on the downs.

ENTRANCE TO BATHAMPTON STATION around 1905. There is a covered footbridge over the tracks at the bottom of the lane.

BATHAMPTON STATION around 1906. The bridge in the centre was used for carrying farm animals to the fields. The station closed to passengers on 3 October 1966.

VIEW OVER BATHAMPTON in around 1940, showing the Coningsby refreshment room and tobacco shop run by Archibald Stearn.

A VERY HEAVY SNOWFALL in the Warminster Road around 1908.

Bathford

THE ANTIQUE ROOMS AND ROOF GARDEN, run by Mrs E. Lavington, at the Crown Inn, Bathford around 1912. This was the Bathford tram terminus. The parish of Bathford is the third largest surrounding the city of Bath, with approximately 1,800 acres and a population of around 1,800 people.

THE BUS AT BATHFORD, dropping passengers for the Bath bound tram in around 1910.

THE BARE HILLS OF BROWN'S FOLLY in around 1912.

LONDON ROAD, Bathford around 1905, with the eighteenth-century New Inn at the top. Children have stopped playing with their hoops and skipping ropes to pose for the photographer.

BATHFORD HILL in around 1908.

LOOKING DOWN BATHFORD HILL around 1930.

BATHFORD in around 1908. A.J. Maslen's general store opened in 1901. In 1909 it became Maslen's and Sons and traded as such for many years. On the left is the Smiths Arms.

BATHFORD SCHOOLS in around 1905.

BATHFORD POST OFFICE in around 1910.

CHURCH STREET, Bathford around 1906. Leonard's grocery shop is on the right.

FURTHER ALONG CHURCH STREET around 1906.

THE FIRST STEAM LORRY IN BATHFORD was owned by Frank Lavington, who ran his haulage business from the Crown Inn.

THE HUT TEA GARDENS at Bathford Hill. The owner, Mrs Prince, lived here from 1937.

SECTION THIRTEEN

Freshford and Limpley Stoke

THE VIADUCT HOTEL around 1912.

THE LIMPLEY STOKE VIADUCT around 1906.

THE DUNDAS AQUEDUCT around 1920. It was built in 1810 to carry the canal over the river Avon.

A GENERAL VIEW OF LIMPLEY STOKE VALLEY in around 1928.

THE HOP POLE at Limpley Stoke, selling Symonds Ales, in around 1935.

LIMPLEY STOKE in around 1930.

THE ROSE AND CROWN at Limpley Stoke in 1911.

MRS BOWLES' TEA GARDENS at Murhill. These were officially called The Strawberry Gardens from 1898 to 1920.

ENTRANCE TO THE WOODS AT LIMPLEY STOKE in around 1908.

FRESHFORD MILL at Staples Hill around 1905.

THE RED TRIANGLE CLUB at Freshford.

FRESHFORD POST OFFICE around 1920.

A SCENIC VIEW ALONG THE CANAL at Limpley Stoke.

Monkton Combe

VIEW OVER LIMPLEY STOKE FROM BRASSKNOCKER HILL around 1912.

MONKTON COMBE in around 1905.

MONKTON COMBE in around 1912. The church nestling in the corner was built in 1865 after many others had fallen into disrepair on this site.

A PICTURESQUE VIEW OF MILL LANE, Monkton Combe around 1912.

MONKTON COMBE in around 1912.

THE CROWN INN, Brassknocker Hill, known as the Old Brassknocker Inn. The inn was turned into cottages early this century.

THE SWIMMING POOL AT MONKTON COMBE SCHOOL around 1948.

MONKTON COMBE JUNIOR SCHOOL around 1920. The new building was built in 1907. The old school was at Combe Lodge.

MONKTON COMBE SCHOOL around 1904. It was started as a private school in 1868 by the Reverend Francis Pocock. The Limpley Stoke viaduct is in the background.

THE FARM, part of the Monkton Combe School.

Combe Down and Claverton

THE AVENUE, COMBE DOWN, showing the Hadley Arms Hotel, in around 1903. The proprietor was F. M. Flower, and the Bath Brewery supplied the ale.

THE VILLAGE, COMBE DOWN around 1906, with the post office on the right. Combe Down village was started in 1729 when Ralph Allen built eleven workmen's cottages.

THE TRAM HEADING FOR BATH around 1906.

THE CAPTION reads 'Chaves Tea Gardens, Combe Down', but this is more likely to be Blakes Farm at Englishcombe in around 1905.

THE AVENUE, Combe Down around 1906.

CHURCH ROAD, Combe Down around 1912.

SUMMER LANE, Combe Down around 1906.

THE CARRIAGE DRIVE, situated above Lyncombe, was the private drive to Prior Park estate.

THE TRAM ARRIVING FROM BATH at Rainbow Woods in 1938.

PRIOR PARK, Bath around 1912. The mansion was designed and built for Ralph Allen by John Wood. The church was built later, in 1844, and there have been many alterations to the buildings since then. Prior Park is now a boys' and girls' boarding and day school.

THE PALLADIUM BRIDGE around 1912. It was built in 1755 within the beautiful grounds of Prior Park. This view shows the lake at the bottom and Widcombe church nestling in the background.

WESTBURY AVENUE, Combe Down around 1912, showing M. A. Ponting, the stationers which housed the post office.

ONE OF THE BATH STONE QUARRIES at Combe Down around 1904.

CLAVERTON VILLAGE around 1908.

COPELAND, on the Claverton Downs, around 1915.

SECTION SIXTEEN

Southstoke, Midford and Combe Hay

SOUTHSTOKE in around 1920. This is the view from Brewery Cottage.

SOUTHSTOKE in around 1920.

THE BUTCHERS SHOP AND POST OFFICE in the centre of Southstoke around 1906.

THE TYTHE BARN, Southstoke around 1920.

SOUTHSTOKE in around 1920, showing Brewery Cottage and the brewery which closed in 1910 and has since been pulled down.

A VIEW OVER SOUTHSTOKE VILLAGE around 1915.

THE HOPE AND ANCHOR, Midford, thought to have been called the White Hart. The name was changed when the Somerset Coal Canal was built in 1800. The proprietor, Tom Darke, was there after 1935 and the licence stayed with the family until the 1950s.

A STEAM DELIVERY LORRY, C. 1910, for the Fullers Earth Union Ltd, which operated on the old Somerset Coal Canal near Midford from 1880.

THE OLD WATERMILL at Midford around 1904, now a private residence.

our hut was underneath thi. "

THE RAILWAY BRIDGE at Midford around 1905.

A GENERAL VIEW OF MIDFORD around 1905, with the station in the background. The station is now closed.

A LOVELY DISPLAY OF HATS at the Midford flower show in 1912.

A GENERAL VIEW OVER COMBE HAY in around 1925.

COMBE HAY VILLAGE POST OFFICE in 1907. The young lady with her bicycle stands on the village green.

SECTION SEVENTEEN

Englishcombe

A QUIET LANE AT ENGLISHCOMBE around 1921. Englishcombe is said to have been a residence of the Saxon kings and was a manor belonging to de Gournay, one of the murderers of Edward II. On his execution, his estates were confiscated and Englishcombe passed to the Duchy of Cornwall, the Prince of Wales now being the lord of the manor.

ENGLISHCOMBE TEA GARDENS in around 1906.

PICTURESQUE COTTAGES at Englishcombe in around 1915.

ENGLISHCOMBE in around 1915.

THE PRINCE OF WALES at Englishcombe village on 18 July 1923. He visited the Duchy Manors after visiting Bath. He was approached to donate some land for a village hall. He did so, and also donated a sum of money for the building fund.

THE POST OFFICE AND BAKERS in Englishcombe village around 1906.

THE OLD TYTHE BARN at Englishcombe around 1906.

Newton St Loe and Corston

The Tram Terminus, Newton Saint Loe.

M. J. R. — B. No 2521

THE TRAM TERMINUS AT NEWTON ST LOE around 1905. The last tram ran from here in October 1938, a year earlier than in Bath.

THE CENTRE OF NEWTON ST LOE VILLAGE in around 1906.

NEWTON ST LOE around 1915 with the village hall in the background.

STOPPING FOR A PHOTOGRAPH at Newton Bridge in 1905. The first Bath bus, filled with the tramway's employees, on a test run. In 1905 twelve buses were purchased by the Bath Electric Tramways Co. Ltd to transport passengers from the Glasshouse terminus and the Bathford terminus to outlying districts. In 1920 the Bath Tramway Motor Company was formed to take over the motor business.

THE POST OFFICE in Newton St Loe around 1905. Perhaps the bicycle parked outside belonged to the postman.

THE POST OFFICE AT CORSTON in 1904. It was run by the Salmon family from 1870 until 1963 when it closed. Mr Eric Salmon still occupies the house. It was the last post office in the eastern district of Bristol.

CORSTON VILLAGE in around 1915. The village stores and bakery was run by the Harrill family at this time, Mrs Harrill also doubling as the village schoolmistress. Now a private house, the building contains a sixteenth-century bacon-curing chamber. The village post office was here from 1963 to 1973.

R. C. HARRILL'S BAKER'S VAN outside the Wheatsheaf Inn at Corston around 1912. The Douglas brothers are shown on the motorbikes which they manufactured in Kingswood from 1907.

Corston Village, Nr. Bath.

M. J. R. — B. No 2500

THE MAIN ROAD THROUGH CORSTON in around 1902.

BROOK VIEW, CORSTON.

BROOK VIEW, CORSTON, which has now been restored, around 1915.

Dunkerton and Wellow

DUNKERTON STATION around 1915. The station closed on 21 September 1925.

DUNKERTON COLLIERY around 1915. The miners were handed their notices on 30 August 1927 and the pit closed on 6 September of the same year.

THE FORD AT WELLOW around 1950.

WELLOW STATION in around 1904. It closed on 7 March 1966.

THE WATER TROUGH in the centre of Wellow in around 1912. It is in memory of William Cole, a local farmer who cared for the poor and needy, and was given by his friends in 1907.